Your First Orchid

LOUISE HARVEY

ISBN-10: 1514223481
ISBN-13: 978-1514223482

CONTENTS

INTRODUCTION

Orchids are one of the most popular houseplants around today. They possess great beauty that can be appreciated by anyone. To single them out for their beauty would be unfair, because they offer so much more than that. They're a complicated flower and they're full of contradictions. They grow just about anywhere in the world, and they have an odd mix of toughness and fragility. They require very specific environmental conditions to grow, and a completely different set of requirements to bloom.

I've experienced my share of joys and frustrations growing this gorgeous flower. I've read numerous books, talked to experienced growers and watched many tutorials on how to grow and care for them. I've experimented with what I've learned and had a mixture of outcomes. I've produced beautiful flowers that have bloomed for over four months, and others which failed to bloom at all. Through my years of learning, experience, and trial & error I've been able to replicate the long blooms and reduce the amount of premature losses. I've shared my knowledge with friends and family and they've also profited from significant blooms. With the right knowledge they can last a long time, with little maintenance.

I decided to write this book to help guide complete beginners on how to grow, care for, and ultimately understand the wonderful Orchid. This book is designed to help someone with no, or very little knowledge on the subject, to understand the different types of Orchids, the easiest types to grow, which tools I've found most useful, the conditions you need to influence its growth, how to pot or repot your Orchid, which pests and diseases to look out for, why you might not experience a bloom, and my top tips to Orchid success. At the end of the book I've provided some resources that I've found useful to take my knowledge and understanding to a new level.

I hope you enjoy this guide and take pleasure from your time cultivating this fabulous flower.

INTRODUCTION TO ORCHIDS

As part of the flowering plant family, known by the scientific name of Orchidaceae, orchids are revered worldwide for their beauty, fragrance and symmetrical perfection.

Orchids have been coveted since first seen by Europeans centuries ago. In fact, during the 1800's, orchid hunters often set out from Europe to travel to the tropics and bring back these precious plants.

Perhaps one of the most famous of these orchid hunters was Benedict Roezel, who alone accounted for bringing over 800 species of never before seen plants, trees and orchids back to Europe.

Roezel did his hunting for Frederick Sandler, a German nursery owner who became one of the world's leading orchid experts of the time.

Today there are around 25,000 to 30,000 discovered species of orchids found worldwide.

Other interesting orchid facts

Before we learn more about growing your own orchid, let's look at a few more interesting facts about them.

- **Orchid symmetry is similar to that of the human face**

  Orchids and the faces of human share a common bond in that they have bilateral symmetry. What exactly does that mean? Well, if a line was drawn straight down the flower vertically, the left and right side are exact mirror images. This also occurs in humans and maybe explains why we love orchids so much.

- **Orchids utilize deception**

Often the reproductive section of an orchid is both in the shape and color of the insect they need to attract for pollination. If the insect lands on the orchid it collects the pollen and eventually flies off to another orchid thus helping the pollination process.

- **Vanilla**

  Do you love the taste of vanilla? Ever wondered where vanilla beans originate from? They come from a climbing orchid called *Vanilla Planifolia*. Local tribes in Central America used the bean from this plant as a flavoring. The flower itself was introduced into Europe in the 1500's.

- **Orchids have many uses**

  The tribes of both Central and South America used orchid roots to make glue by drying them out in the sun, smashing them into a powder and finally adding water. Orchids are also used for their medicinal qualities by many cultures in curing coughs, headaches and fevers.

Orchids are truly amazing flowers and not only for their stunning beauty.

THE ORCHID FAMILY

Orchids are amazing plants able to live and thrive in every type of ecosystem except for deserts, glaciers and vast expanses of water.

Most orchids are found in tropical areas however.

There are two distinct types of orchids which grow quite differently to each other. Knowing how each type grows will help you determine the best for you and how to grow them. These two types of orchids are:

- **Terrestrial orchids**

  These orchids are grown in the ground and flourish in soil. They do not produce any aerial roots at all. They are also able to withstand the cold extremely well, making them a perfect orchid for slightly colder climates.

- **Epiphyte orchids**

  They are often called "air plants" because they grow on other plants, mostly for support and are not parasitic in any way. This category includes many of the orchids found today. This gives the orchid a chance to grow without any surrounding competition and brings them closer to the light, which they need to thrive.

  These orchids need their roots exposed to air in order for them to grow correctly. They prefer humid areas to enhance their growth and to stop their roots from drying out. These are the easiest orchids to grow indoors and the orchid you choose will in all likelihood be an epiphyte orchid.

Orchids are further grouped into two categories by the way that they grow. These are:

- **Monopodial orchids**

  These orchids are characterized by a single stem that grows upright. The leaves of the orchid grow opposite each other on each side of the stem. The flower itself will appear at the top of the stem, above the uppermost leaves.

- **Sympodial orchids**

  These orchids are more common and grow horizontally by sending out shoots from the initial rhizome. Leaves and flowers then appear at the top of these shoots. These orchids often form swollen shoots called pseudobulbs which store water and nutrients.

The three easiest orchids to grow indoors are:

- **Lady slipper orchid**

  These orchids are small to medium in size. They have beautiful flowers which are often mottled and last very long after blooming. They prefer lower light.

- **Cattleya orchid**

  These orchids are small to medium in size. They have extremely bright and colorful flowers. They require filtered bright light.

- **Moth orchid**

  These orchids are medium in size and have small, medium and large flowers in a variety of colors that bloom for long periods.

Like Cattleya orchids, they need filtered light.

ORCHID TOOLS

To successfully grow your orchid, you will need a number of tools and other supplies. Most of these items you will either have at home already or be able to purchase relatively inexpensively.

Let's have a look at each item in closer detail to see exactly how it will be used during the growth and care of your orchid.

- **Cutting Tool**

  At some point you will need to remove rotten roots and dead leaves from your orchid. A small garden shears, pruner or floral scissors would work perfectly for this task. Please note, whatever tool you choose, it must be sterilized after use. Although there are various ways to do this, using rubbing alcohol is the easiest. Take either cotton balls or paper towels, soak in the rubbing alcohol and wipe the cutting tool. Rinse with water and dry. This helps to prevent the spread of diseases between plants.

- **Orchid Fertilizer**

  Fertilizer is essential to help your orchid grow. There are various different kinds available, so make sure that you get the correct one for the orchid type you are growing. If unsure, you can purchase a general fertilizer with a 20-20-20 nutrient ratio which can be used on a majority of orchids.

- **Spray Bottle**

  In all probability, you will have one of these at home already. Use this to spray your plant in between regular watering times. This is extremely important if you live in a location with high humidity. Spray the orchid all over, including all visible roots. Roots which grow outside the pot are often the first to dry out, quickly affecting the health of your orchid.

- **Humidity Tray**

  This is particularly useful if you live in a very dry region and your orchid is not receiving enough humidity. These can be purchased from all nurseries or you could even make your own by placing rocks and smaller stones into a bowl. Add some water to the bottom and place your orchid pot on top of the rocks and stones. Make sure the bottom of the pot does not touch the water. As the water evaporates it will create humidity for your orchid.

- **Humidity Gauge**

  A humidity gauge will allow you to measure the humidity around your orchid, thus allowing you to adjust it if necessary so your orchid can thrive.

- **Stakes**

  Although not essential, a stake can help to ensure that your orchid is presented standing upright in all its beauty. Stakes can also be used to provide support for your orchid if needed, especially if you are transporting your orchid, perhaps to its first show!

- **Clips**

  These are used to help secure the orchid stems to the stake or to help secure the orchid if it is unsteady after repotting.

CARING FOR YOUR ORCHID

Now that you know exactly what tools you will need to help you care for your orchid, we will look at other aspects that will influence its growth.

Various factors will determine how well your orchid will grow and bloom. These include light, temperature, humidity, air movement, watering, pruning and fertilizers.

Let's take a look at each one in closer detail.

- **Light**

  Orchids love light but the amount of light needed does differ from Orchid to Orchid. A general guideline is that orchids should receive around 12 to 14 hours of light each day. Often securing enough natural sunlight for an orchid will sometimes become a problem during winter but this problem can be solved by using artificial light. You can position the orchid around 6 to 8 inches away from a set of 4 foot long fluorescent lights and they should suffice during winter if no sunshine is present.

  The color of the orchid's leaves is a good indication whether the orchid is receiving the correct amount of light. Orchid leaves should be bright green in color. If they are dark green they are getting too little light and yellow leaves indicate the orchid is receiving too much light.

- **Temperature**

  Orchids are able to bloom by producing energy during the day when temperatures are higher and storing the energy at night when temperatures are lower. The fluctuation between the day and night time temperature (around 10-15 degrees Fahrenheit) is paramount in helping an orchid bloom.

You should aim for a day time temperature of around 75 to 80 degrees Fahrenheit and a night time temperature of between 60 – 62 degrees Fahrenheit.

- **Humidity**

  Orchids are very partial to humidity and it plays a very important part in getting your orchid to bloom each year.

  An ideal humidity range during the day is around 50% to 70%. Depending on your location, the humidity level may drop below this during summer.

  Using a humidity tray can help to keep the humidity at the required level. Place your orchid on the tray but never let the water in the tray touch the bottom of your orchid pot.

  Another option is a misting the orchid a few times a day using a spray bottle depending how dry the climate is.

- **Air movement**

  Air movement is also important for orchids. A small overhead fan set to the slowest speed will provide the perfect amount of air movement for your orchid. Another option is a normal oscillating fan that is facing away from the orchid. Remember to leave the fans running at night as well.

  If your orchid is in a high humidity area you should increase the air movement. This is especially true at night time when high humidity without much air movement can promote fungal growth.

  Moving air is also important in keeping leaf temperature down.

- **Watering**

Watering your orchid is in no way similar to watering another house-plant. There are many factors to consider when watering including the water quality, the temperature of the water, the best time to water and how often the orchid type needs to be watered.

Over-watering an orchid causes the roots to be submerged in the water. If this water is not drained, the roots will eventually rot. Under watering can lead to the roots of the orchid drying up. It is a fine balance, but easily learned.

Water quality is also very important. Water with impurities can be detrimental to an orchid as it can block the pores on the orchid's leaves. If you are unsure, boil the water first before using it. Ensure you use room temperature water when watering your orchid and allow any excess water to drain away. Always water the orchid in the morning thus allowing time for the root system to dry out and not retain water. Never water at night.

Finally, the most often asked question. When should an orchid be watered? One of the easiest ways to determine this depends on the pot type you have placed the orchid in. If you have used a clay pot, you will need to water more frequently as clay allows water to evaporate quicker than a plastic pot. Another factor is your potting mix. If your potting mix has water retention aspects to it, you need to water less frequently and vice versa. We look at pot types and potting mix in closer detail in a later chapter.

There are a few simple methods that you can use to see if your orchid needs to be watered. When you water your plant, pick it up and feel its weight. Do this each time you water your plant and soon you will know just by picking up the orchid in its pot whether it needs water or not. Alternatively, place your finger in the potting mix. Remove your finger and if it is damp then the orchid does not require watering.

A general rule is that you will water your orchid every 7 to 10 days.

- **Pruning**

  Pruning your orchid is a very important part in getting it to bloom each year. Orchids normally bloom from around February and March in the northern hemisphere. A bloom can last anything from four to twelve weeks. Once the blooming is over, cut off the spike at around ½ inch from where it comes out of the foliage. This will encourage new growth in the spike. If the spike has bloomed a number of seasons and you have other spikes emerging you may choose to cut the spike about one inch above the potting mix. Blooming from the same spike over and over can damage the plant. If your plant has no other new spikes, cut it in the way mentioned above to encourage new growth.

  Trim any dead leaves and old flower stems at this point as well. Always remember to use sterile cutting tools.

- **Fertilizers**

  Orchids grown at home will need fertilizers to help stimulate healthy growth. If your plant is in poor condition, fertilizers will not solve the problem. You will need to find what is causing the problem and fix it.

  Only use a fertilizer that is made for use with orchids. These fertilizers are made up mostly out of potassium, nitrogen and phosphorus. Let's look at how each of these benefits an orchid.

  Potassium helps your orchid grow. Not getting enough potassium will cause slow growth in an orchid. Nitrogen helps with stem and leaf growth. Beware however, too much nitrogen and your orchid will grow too large and take time to flower.

Phosphorous helps with flower production and root growth.

The combination of these chemicals in your fertilizer is often dependant on what potting mix you have used. If you are unsure, ask your local nursery, but generally using a 20-20-20 ratio of potassium, nitrogen and phosphorus should work.

Fertilizers come in various forms including water soluble, granules and slow-release formulas. Slow-release and granules can be applied to your potting mix. If you add too much they can burn the orchid's roots. The easiest to use is water soluble fertilizers.

ORCHID POTS, POTTING MATERIAL AND RE-POTTING YOUR ORCHID

In this chapter, we will be looking at the various orchid pots/containers available to you, the potting material you will need when re-potting your orchid and finally we will look at how to re-pot your orchid.

Choosing your pot/container

There are a few things that you need to look at when deciding on the pot for your orchid.

- **Size required**

To determine the size of the pot your orchid will require, you will need to look at the diameter of the pot itself, which is usually measured in inches. The secret here is to select a pot that is only slightly bigger than the roots of your orchid.

- **Type of Pot**

There are many different pots for you to choose from.

The most affordable and most chosen option is a regular plastic pot. Make sure the pot has drainage holes and that it will not heat up too much in direct sunlight as this will be detrimental to the orchid. These sometimes even come in a clear variety which allows you to see the roots of your orchid with ease as well as allowing more light to penetrate to the roots. Treat clear pots with a coating of UV blocker to help stop the pot degrading easily.

Clay/Terracotta pots tend to look more stylish than a regular plastic pot and are often used for this reason alone. They are also much more stable than a plastic pot. They normally have one large drainage hole in the bottom of the pot. Take note, water evaporates far quicker from a clay pot and if you chose to use this pot for your orchids you will need to check if your orchid has enough water more often.

- Decorative pots are also tempting to use because of how they compliment the beauty of the orchid. Unfortunately, these pots have often been treated with a glaze that can harm your orchid. If you want to use a pot like this then place it in a plastic or ceramic pot first before placing it in the decorative pot.

Baskets made from either wooden slats or plastic nets can also be used as a container for your orchid. Some form of layering should be used to prevent the potting material from falling out. Sheet moss is normally perfect for this. These containers help to allow air to circulate around the roots of the orchid. Orchids in basket containers are prone to drying out and must be monitored thoroughly.

Perhaps the most important thing to remember when choosing a pot for your orchids is that it is there to help encourage an environment similar from which the orchid would have come from in nature.

Potting material

Orchids are very different to other plants when it comes to the correct mix of materials for potting. Orchids need a mix that will provide enough air to the roots of the plant as well as allowing water retention. This ratio is determined by the type of orchid species you are growing.

Potting material that will encourage orchid growth is usually a combination of organic fibres and inorganic materials. You can either buy these already mixed or you can make your own.

Organic materials comprise the following:

- **Coconut Husks**

These are extremely cheap, have acceptable water retention properties but the husks decay quickly. These were the first fibers to be used as potting mix for orchids

- **Sphagnum Moss**

This provides a very good balance of both water and air retention but must not be packed together too tightly.

- **Tree Fern Fiber**

These have slow decomposition rates with excellent drainage properties.

- **Fir Bark**

This is cheap and relatively easy to find. It will decompose slowly but has difficulty holding water at first.

- **Redwood Bark**

This bark decomposes slower than fir bark and has far better water retention properties.

Inorganic materials comprise the following:

- **Lava Rock**

This will never decompose and offers excellent drainage

- **Charcoal**

This decays extremely slowly while it has the ability to absorb toxic substances

- **Alifor**

These are little pieces of clay that will never decompose while providing moderate drainage.

- **Vermiculite**

This provides excellent aeration by retaining water

- **Pearlite**

Pearlite has high water absorption properties. It must be used in conjunction with other inorganic materials for this reason.

- **Turface**

This is very expensive. Can be used in place of Pearlite but it is much heavier.

Your potting mix should be a combination of 70 – 85 % organic material and the rest made up by inorganic materials. Remember to ask yourself a couple of questions to determine the best mix to use.

- What size is my orchid?

- Does it like more or less moisture?

Here are a few simple mixes you can make yourself. Remember, your local nursery will be able to make this up for you if you feel the task might be too complicated.

- **Large size orchids with dry root requirements**

This mix should comprise 80% coarse grade fir bark, redwood bark or tree fern fiber and 20% coarse grade charcoal or lava rock.

- **Large size orchids with moist root requirements**

This mix should comprise 80% sphagnum or coconut husk, 15% coarse grade charcoal or lava rock and 5% vermiculite.

- **Medium size orchids with dry root requirements**

This mix should comprise 80% medium grade fir bark, redwood bark or tree fern fiber and 20% medium grade charcoal or lava rock.

- **Medium size orchids with moist root requirements**

This mix should comprise 80% sphagnum or coconut husk, 15% medium grade charcoal or lava rock and 5% vermiculite.

- **Miniature orchids with dry root requirements**

This mix should comprise 80% fine grade fir bark, redwood bark or tree fern fiber and 20% fine grade charcoal or lava rock.

- **Miniature size orchids with moist root requirements**

This mix should comprise 80% sphagnum or coconut husk, 15% fine grade charcoal or lava rock and 5% vermiculite.

Re-potting your Orchid

At some stage during caring for your orchid you will have to re-pot it. This can seem extremely daunting but it need not be!

When should you re-pot your orchid? These are a few indications that it is time to re-pot.

- The orchid has outgrown its pot.

- The orchid has become top heavy and falls over.

- The orchid has a new shoot growing outside the pot.

- The potting mix needs to be replaced.

- The orchid is unhealthy and the root system needs to be examined.

- The orchid needs dividing.

- The orchid is in an active growth period. This makes it easier for the orchid to re-establish itself in the new potting mix.

Following these steps will ensure success when you re-pot your orchid.

- **Step 1 – Un-potting your orchid**

This process starts 24 hours before removing the orchid from its pot. This is much easier to accomplish if the potting mix is slightly damp, therefore you should water your orchid the day before.

If your orchid is in a clay pot, submerge the whole pot in water for 10 – 15 minutes the day before re-potting. The clay pot itself will absorb much of the water and help dislodge any roots that might have become stuck to the pot.

When taking your orchid out of the pot, knock the outside of the pot in all areas to help loosen up the potting mix. You can then remove the orchid from the pot. Be sure to shake off any of the loose potting mix. If any potting mix remains clinging to the root system, remove it as well.

Inspect the root system for any dead roots and remove them with a sterile cutting tool. Dead roots often look dark and are soft to the touch. Don't be alarmed to find around 1/3 of the roots in a rotting or dead condition. If you find more than this it might be because your orchid needed repotting sooner, the potting mix was of poor quality or the pot your orchid was in was too large for the plant. Trim any yellow leaves on the orchid at the same time.

• Step 2 – Divide the orchid (if necessary)

If you have a large orchid, this might be the time to divide it to get more plants. If you do choose to divide your orchid, never divided it into pieces smaller than three growths as these might take extremely long to develop and therefore are susceptible to various diseases.

• Step 3 – Repotting your orchid

By now you will know which potting mix you should be using for your orchid. If you are unsure, ask your local nursery for help.

You will need to ascertain which part of your orchid is the oldest. This will help you to determine how to position the orchid in the pot. If the oldest part of your orchid is found in the centre then position the orchid in the centre of the pot. If the oldest part of the orchid is found on one side then position the orchid on the side of the pot. This will allow for maximum room for the orchid and its roots to grow and develop in the new pot.

To repot the orchid, hold it in the correct position and the correct height and begin to add your potting mix. Tap the pot as you add the mix to prevent air pockets from forming around the roots. Once you have filled the pot, push down on the potting mix to help secure the orchid in place. Remember to check that the orchid is at the correct height in relation to the pot. Be extremely gentle when placing the orchid in its new pot and during the whole process as roots are easily broken. If a root is broken, determine if the whole root is damaged and not just the outside covering of the root. If the whole root is broken, remove it.

If your orchid has developed aerial roots they can also be placed just below the surface of the potting mix. Just be wary of how much you water the orchid as the aerial roots will need to adjust to the fact that they are now buried.

The plant may sometimes still be slightly unsteady. If this is the case, use clips to secure it to a stake to help it to establish itself in the new pot. Orchids can take three times longer to establish themselves in a new pot if left unsteady.

PESTS AND DISEASES

Orchids are susceptible to numerous diseases. We will look at a few of the more common ones, how to prevent them and more importantly how to overcome them.

- **Bacterial Soft and Brown Rot**

  This appears on the leaves of the orchid as small spots, often surrounded by yellow. If untreated it can rot leaves and roots and eventually spread throughout the whole plant. The infected area often has a foul smell and looks water soaked in appearance.

  To treat this disease, remove the infected area with a sterile cutting tool. Spray the orchid with bactericides or a copper based spray. Clean the growing area of the plant with a 10% bleach mix. Treat all nearby plants as they are diseased and check them frequently.

  This disease is spread by water splashing onto nearby plants therefore do not water from a high position if the disease has contaminated an orchid. The disease enjoys hot and moist areas. Keep the leaves of your orchids dry, reduce temperature and humidity and increase air circulation.

- **Bacterial Brown Spot**

  This appears on the leaves of the orchid as a small, water soaked blister which starts off green in color. The spot enlarges and merges with other spots becoming black or brown in color, dried up and sunken. It can, at times, ooze a liquid. This disease is often found during warm weather.

  To treat this disease, remove the infected area with a sterile cutting tool. Spray the orchid with bactericides or a copper based spray. Clean the growing area of the plant with a 10% bleach mix. Treat all nearby plants as they are diseased and check them frequently.

This bacteria is carried in water and thrives in warm, moist conditions. Reduce the temperature and humidity and increase air circulation. Do not water your orchids from overhead.

- **Black Rot**

This appears on the leaves, roots or growth shoots of the orchid. If found on leaves it will be on the underside of the leaf as a small, watery brown spot which quickly change to purple/brown or purple/black. The spots sometimes have a yellow outline. If black rot spreads to other parts of the orchid they will appear with purple/black marks as well.

Treatment is extremely difficult and Black Rot could destroy all your orchids. Isolate the infected orchid and treat with a fungicide. Sometimes the best course of action is to destroy the plant.

Black rot enjoys high temperatures and humidity. Use a fungicide spray to help prevent the disease.

- **Fungal Root Rot**

This disease can happen due to poor drainage or overwatering the orchid. Root rot also occurs from damaged roots, salt build up or overwatering. Sometime root rot can be noticed by the leaves and pseudobulb of orchids becoming yellow, thin, twisted and shrivelled up.

To treat this disease, remove the infected roots and leaves with a sterile cutting tool. Place the orchid in a fungicide and clean the growing area of the plant with a 10% bleach mix.

To prevent root rot keep your potting mix fresh and do not overwater.

Indoor orchids are also susceptible to pests that affect other houseplants. Let's have a closer look at these.

- **Mealybug**

    These white bugs attach themselves to the orchid and suck nutrients from it. To treat the orchid, spray it with a 70% rubbing alcohol solution every 10 to 14 days to kill any emerging bugs. Remove old leaves and flower sheathes where the bugs might hide.

- **Spidermites**

    These small creatures feed on the underside of the leaves of your orchid and are red and brown in color. To treat the orchid, spray it with a miticide.

- **Thrips**

    These small insects feed on flowers and leaves. To treat the orchid, spray it with a pesticide.

If you notice any strange marks or creatures on your orchid and you are unsure what they are, take the orchid to your local nursery. Better to be safe than sorry!

ORCHIDS THAT WILL NOT BLOOM

Despite your loving attention, the best pots money can buy, fertilizers and proper care, your orchid will not bloom. Why is this?

For orchids to bloom, there are numerous factors that need to be in alignment. Let's look at a few things that could be causing the orchid to remain dormant.

- **Light condition**

  Check the lighting conditions in which your orchid finds itself. Is it getting too little light or even too much light? If your orchid is one that requires much light you can help to encourage it to bloom by putting it into a hanging basket and hanging it outside on a tree branch.

  If your orchid receives light from an artificial source make sure that they are switched off to help simulate a day/night cycle which will help encourage the orchid to grow and bloom.

  A great way to determine if your orchid is getting the correct light is to look at its leaves. They should be a beautiful shiny green. If the orchid is getting too little light, the leaves will be dark green and if it is getting too much light, the leaves will be yellowish.

- **Roots**

  An orchid with good roots will generally bloom. Be sure to check the roots of the orchid every time you repot. Also remember to replace the potting mix every time it nears the end of its life cycle.

  As we learnt earlier, overwatering can lead to rotten roots and an unhealthy plant.

- **Temperature**

  Check that there is at least a 10-15 degrees Fahrenheit temperature differential between the day and night time temperature. If there is not, this is one of the reasons the orchid is not blooming.

- **Fertilizer**

  If you are not using a fertilizer on your orchid, it may be lacking in nutrients and that could be causing it not to bloom.

- **Correct season**

  If you bought your orchid in bloom from a nursery it does not mean that that is the correct time for it to bloom. It might have been made to bloom by the nursery at that point to encourage its sale.

- **Re-potting**

  Some orchids will not bloom for up to six months after re-potting as they re-establish themselves in their new pot.

PROVEN TIPS FOR ORCHID CARE

Growing orchids requires much time, patience and care from your part, but the experience of your orchid blooming, its beauty and incredible fragrance will be your reward.

Our last chapter deals with proven tips which will help you in your quest for the perfect orchid. Keeping these factors in mind will help you to make a success out of growing your first orchid and hopefully in years to come, you will have many more!

Know your orchid

When buying your first orchid, be sure that it is one that is suitable for beginners. There is no pointing buying an incredibly beautiful orchid that is currently in bloom by the nursery, but you will have no chance to make it bloom again as it has very specific requirements that you will not be able to provide.

Start off with an orchid that is easy to grow, easy to care for, adaptable to most conditions it might be placed in.

Remember to do your research beforehand. Ask yourself a few questions.

- In which area of the house will the orchid be placed?

- Are the light conditions in this area perfect for the orchid?

- Are the day and night time temperature variations in this area perfect for the orchid? Remember, one of the main requirements for an orchid to bloom is a 10 to 15 degree Fahrenheit variance between day and night time temperatures.

- How much water will your orchid need?

- Is the air circulation sufficient in the area where the orchid will be placed?

- Is the humidity level in the area where the orchid will be placed within the range the orchid requires?

- Once you have the right spot, do not move your orchid unnecessarily.

is a storage organ found in epiphytic & terrestrial sympodial orchids

Choose a healthy orchid

thickening of the part of a stem between leaf nodes

When purchasing your orchid be sure to study the plant thoroughly. Check for signs of any diseases or pest. Be sure to check the leaves, pseudobulbs and the stem of the orchid. Try to see the conditions of any roots (if possible). If the plant has a few pseudobulbs, make sure they are all of a similar size.

Try to buy your orchid that has already bloomed or is currently in bloom at the time of purchase. This means the orchid has had a growth cycle and if you provide the correct conditions for it, it will bloom easily again.

Check the orchid will have enough space to flourish

Take space into consideration when deciding on an orchid. Some orchids need a lot of space as they grow and spread out. You might have the perfect area in terms of light, temperature, humidity and air circulation, but buying an orchid that will end up too big for the area will not work.

Re-potting

At some stage you will need to re-pot your orchid as they have extremely fast growing root systems. If you do not re-pot when the orchid's root system has outgrown its pot, the continued growth of the orchid will stagnate and the orchid roots may begin to rot.

Re-potting might seem daunting but if you follow the process you will find it to be a relatively easy task.

Divide your orchid

Divide your orchid into smaller plants if it has become too large. This will encourage growth and provide you with more blooms. Only do this when your orchid needs to be divided, is mature and has gone through a couple of blooming cycles. If new growths on your orchid have reached the top of the pot and all the above requirements are met, you may divide the plant.

Fertilize

Fertilizing your orchid helps it to receive the nutrients it needs. Fertilize every week with a weak mixture (as discussed earlier). For one week every month, do not fertilize! This will help to wash away any salt build up that might damage the orchid.

Keep a record

Keep records of everything regarding your orchid. Temperatures, humidity levels, how often you water etc. If your orchid flourishes you will have a record of how to replicate that. If you are having problems with the orchid, you can show your records to an expert at a nursery and they can provide advice on what you may have done wrong.

SUMMARY

We are drawn to Orchids because of their natural beauty, their incredible colorful flowers and the amazing aroma that they produce.

I hope you now feel that you're equipped with the basic understanding of how you can grow your own orchids by following the advice outlined in this guide. It will require much planning and research before you purchase them, much patience when growing them and sometimes you will have to overcome disappointment when things go wrong. Don't be deterred.

This is all part of what makes growing an orchid fun! If you hang in there, follow the advice, ask questions of others and care for your orchid, you will be rewarded with the most beautiful flowers.

Of all the traits you will need to call on as an orchid grower, perhaps the one you should have in abundance is patience!

Good luck, may your orchids grow and bloom and fill your house with beauty!

RESOURCES

The following websites are the main ones I referred to and will help you with Orchid growing.

- **Hydro Orchids**

  http://www.hydro-orchids.com/orchid-care-beginner-basics.html

- **Everything Orchids**

  http://everything-orchids.com/

- **Beautiful Orchids**

  http://www.beautifulorchids.com/orchids/orchid_care_tips/orchid_introduction/orchid_care_tips.html

- **Orchid Care Lady**

  http://www.orchidcarelady.com/

I recommend the following books for more information on understanding and caring for Orchids.

- **Taylor's Guide to Orchids**

  http://www.amazon.com/gp/product/0395677262

- **Flora's Orchids**

  http://www.amazon.com/gp/product/088192721X

- **Understanding Orchids**

  http://www.amazon.com/gp/product/0618263268

ABOUT THE AUTHOR

Louise Harvey has been gardening for most of her life. She initially spent time in the garden to be close to her mother, but it wasn't long before she had got the bitten by the gardening bug herself.

Her mother gave her a corner of the garden to look after and she used her patch to grow flowers and vegetables. Once she had used up all of the space, she started filling up her bedroom with house plants and taking over the rest of the family home. Louise's mum gradually gave me more space to work with in the garden and eventually shared the entire backyard with her.

She hasn't stopped since. The main difference now is that she has her own home and garden to work on, and her mother has her own one back.

Louise vows to continue learning and experimenting in the garden for as long as possible. She enjoys trying out new methods for optimal growth and isn't afraid to make mistakes along the way. She confesses to making thousands of mistakes in her time in the garden, and she's keen to pass on what she's learned to amateur gardeners alike.

Gardening has changed her life forever. She finds it relaxing, fun, and hugely rewarding. She would like everyone to discover the same benefits.

She's helped numerous friends, family members and colleagues with their home and garden, and she wants to reach out to help more people. Her books are quick reference guides that are simple to understand, fun to read, and provide the amateur gardener with the basic information they need to start gardening.

OTHER BOOKS BY LOUISE HARVEY

Air Plants - A Beginners Guide To Understanding Air Plants, Growing Air Plants and Air Plant Care

Your First Cacti - A Beginners Guide To Cacti and Succulents

Your First Bonsai - A Beginners Guide To Bonsai Growing, Bonsai Care, and Understanding The Bonsai

Composting - The Complete Guide To Composting and Creating Your Own Compost

Self Sufficient Living - A Beginners Guide To Self Sufficient Living and Homesteading

Made in the USA
Columbia, SC
03 March 2019